FRUIT OF THE SPIRIT

M000008133

LOVE

Fruit of the Spirit Study Guide Series

Love

Joy

Peace

Patience

Kindness

Goodness

Faithfulness

Gentleness

Self-Control

CALVIN MILLER

FRUIT OF THE SPIRIT

LOVE

Published in Nashville, Tennessee, by Thomas Nelson. Thomas Nelson is a trademark of Thomas Nelson, Inc.

Thomas Nelson, Inc., titles may be purchased in bulk for educational, business, fund-raising, or sales promotional use. For information, please e-mail SpecialMarkets@ThomasNelson.com.

Typesetting by Gregory C. Benoit Publishing, Old Mystic, CT.

ISBN: 978-1-4185-2841-6

Printed in the United States of America
08 09 10 11 12 RRD 9 8 7 6 5 4 3 2 1

TABLE OF CONTENTS

But the fruit of the Spirit is love, joy, peace, patience, kindness, goodness, faithfulness, gentleness and self-control.
Against such things there is no law.

—Galatians 5:22–23

INTRODUCTION

It is one of the most misunderstood of all the fruits of the Spirit—love. We love football, apple pie, and our kids. We love shopping, our spouses, and weekends. But does any of this have anything to do with God? We believe that love grows and dies and is something to be sought after. Yet the Bible paints a different picture.

As a by-product of the indwelling of the Holy Spirit, love is a characteristic of God. So there are many things we believe about love that simply aren't true. Love doesn't turn its head to sin. If it did, then God can't love. Love doesn't demand something in return. If so, then we are doomed to live without God's love.

God loves us in spite of our repeated disobedience. It is this kind of love that comes alive in a believer as God squeezes out our selfishness and conceit. Let's be honest, this kind of love is uncommon in today's world. We have grown skeptical of anyone who shows us love. Unconsciously, we can even grow skeptical of God. What does he expect me to do in return for his love, and is it worth it?

God doesn't love us because we are lovable; he loves us because he *is* love. Even when God is angry, he loves us. Even when we turn our backs on him and go our own way, he loves us. He loves us because he can't do anything else.

That's the kind of love that accompanies God's presence in our lives. Paul listed it first because it is a prerequisite for the other fruits of the spirit. Without love, there is no joy, peace, patience, and so on. Without God's love, we can never live up to our God-given potential.

Too many believers are rendered ineffective because they refuse to let God's love work through their lives. They can't forgive because they can't love. They can't experience peace because they can't love. Paul said that claiming to love God while refusing to love others is nothing more than a lot of noise. In this study we'll learn to let God's love come alive in us so that we can come alive for him.

HOW TO USE THIS GUIDE

Galatians 5:22–23 is not a plan to achieve better faith. Rather, it is a description of God's personal gifts to all of us. If we follow God and seek his blessing, then the fruits of the Spirit are a natural overflow in our relationship with God. We are to grow in character so that one day we will reflect the image of our Lord.

This series of nine six-week studies will clearly focus your spiritual life to become more like Christ. Each study guide is divided into six weeks, and each of the six-week courses covers one of the fruits of the Spirit. Participants simply read each daily study and answer the questions at the end of each devotional. This prepares everyone for the group discussion at the end of the week.

Each week features a similar pattern that explores one aspect of that study's fruit of the Spirit. The first lesson establishes the aspect of the fruit to be explored throughout the week. The second lesson looks at the week's theme as it relates to God's purpose in the life of the believer. The third lesson looks at the week's theme as it relates to the believer's relationship with Christ. The fourth lesson explores how the fruit is relevant in service to others. And in the fifth lesson, the theme is related to personal worship. A sixth lesson is included as a bonus study, and focuses on either a biblical character who modeled this particular fruit, or a key parable that brings the theme into focus.

Each weeklong study should conclude in a group review. The weekly group discussion serves as a place to understand the practical side of the theme and receive encouragement and feedback on the journey to become more Christlike. For the study to have the character-transforming effect God desires, it is important for the participant to spend ten to twenty minutes a day reading the Scripture passage and the devotional, and to think through the two questions for the day. If each participant reads all of the questions beforehand, it greatly enhances the group dynamic. Each participant should choose three or four questions to discuss during the group session.

These simple guidelines will help make group time productive. Take a total of about forty-five minutes to answer and discuss the questions. Each person need not answer every question, but be sure all members participate. You can stimulate participation by having everyone respond to an icebreaker question. Have each group member answer the first of the six questions listed at the end of the week, and leave the remaining questions open-ended. Or, make up your own icebreaker question, such as: What color best represents the day you are having? What is your favorite movie? Or, how old were you when you had your first kiss?

No one should respond to all of the questions. Keep in mind that if you are always talking, the others are not. It is essential that everyone contribute. If you notice that someone is not participating, ask that group member which question is the most relevant. Be sensitive if something is keeping that member from contributing. Don't ask someone to read or pray aloud unless you know that the member is comfortable with such a task.

Always start and end your time with prayer. Sometimes it helps to have each person say what he or she plans to do with the lesson that week. Remember to reserve ten minutes for group prayer. You might want to keep a list of requests and answers to prayer at the back of this book.

Week 1: The Evidence of Love Is Giving

Memory Passage for the Week: Psalm 18:1–3

Day 1: The Evidence of Love Is Giving

One only needs to read the first chapter of the book of Genesis to understand how deeply God loves us: he gave us his beautiful creation. Genesis 1:29.

Day 2: The Purpose of God in My Life

Sometimes God's purposes in our lives come to us as a process of slow revelation. Genesis 21:1–6.

Day 3: My Relationship with Christ

One of the grand evidences that God's giving love is operative is that God acted once-and-for-all, in Christ, to forgive all our sins. Romans 4:7–8.

Day 4: My Service to Others

Jesus makes it clear that those who taste God's giving love must see that such grace carries within it the obligation to love others. John 21:15.

Day 5: My Personal Worship

God's love is always there as a motive to praise him. When we are over-whelmed by this love, we can only pause and then burst into hymns of gratitude. Hosea 11:1–8.

Day 6: A Character Study on Ruth

Ruth 1:16–17

Day 7: Group Discussion

Day 1: The Evidence of Love Is Giving

Read Genesis 1:29

The primary evidence of love is giving. There is no surer index of love than that. No wonder Shakespeare said, "He does not love who does not show his love." No sooner were Adam and Eve created than their loving Creator said, "I give you every seed-bearing plant on the face of the whole earth ... they shall be yours!" (Genesis 1:29). Human beings were barely created before they received a gift from God: the earth itself!

One can only imagine "Mr. and Mrs. First Folks" saying, "No, God—it is too much! All of this for us?"

God surely would have replied, "Yes, it is all for you. You must learn in receiving this gift from me that I love you, and that while your descendants may someday think that they can give without loving, no one can ever love without giving. Here on the first day of your existence, receive this present—this planet—as an evidence that I am God and God is love. Then you will know that you were made and given this world because I love you. I am God. My desire toward my children is to keep showing them my love forever."

In the next chapters of Genesis, an unthinkable pageant took place. Adam and Eve disobeyed. Having been loved to the level of Paradise, they abandoned God's love for the empty pleasures of all God had forbidden. The first sin wasn't just bad because it was first; the first sin was bad because it refused to honor the holy, pure love of heaven. This reprehensible treatment of God's love slammed shut the gates of Eden. Not only was Adam's exile *his* punishment, it is the final punishment of *all* those who see the love of God and turn their backs.

The seeds of human desperation lie at every refusal to cherish the most valuable treasure in the world—the love of God.

Questions for Personal Reflection

1. Do you feel loved? By whom?

2. How is that love shown to you?

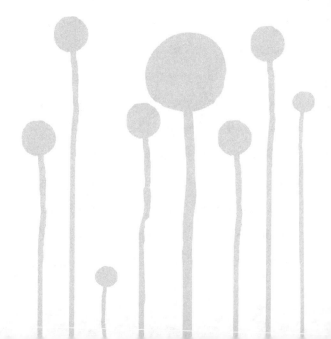

Day 2: The Purpose of God in My Life
Read Genesis 21:1–6

God's giving love is signed and sealed in grace. In fact, the glory of Sarah's life can be summed up in Genesis 21:1–2: "The LORD was gracious to Sarah ... and the LORD did for Sarah what he had promised. Sarah became pregnant." The schedule of God's giving love may, at times, appear to us odd or irrational, but it is not so. Sarah once laughed at the notion of late-in-life motherhood, and named her firstborn Isaac, meaning "laughter." Sarah found during her post-menopausal pregnancy that although God's promises may seem to sleep for a while, they are never comatose.

At an age when older women gaze back across the years at the infancies of their grandchildren, Sarah held her firstborn and easily saw that God is love. And because God is love, his great heart of love compels him to give. So the words *grace* and *gracious* are related, and grace in its most simple meaning is "gift."

When we say "grace" at the dinner table, we thank God for his gifts. If we say a ballerina has grace, we mean she is gifted with poise, balance, and interpretation. If we say God is gracious, or full of grace, we mean he gives gifts to his children—undeserved gifts that enrich us and establish God's giving love in the center of our souls. At the moment of this insight, we are changed forever.

So how are we to view the purpose of God in our lives? God desires that our bodies be the emissaries of communicating his love. Our feet carry his message. Our hands break his living bread. Our minds hold his vision, and our hearts beat with his compassion, all in the name of love.

Sarah's motherhood is one of the best biblical examples that God's love is a dialogue of life. Our mistake is to assume, as Sarah did, that our relationship with God is only a monologue, and that we need to do all the talking. But God is there—in the middle of our lives—and he is neither absent nor silent. When we are silent long enough, God speaks. It is then we discover that he was there all along.

Questions for Personal Reflection

1. Do you know what God's purpose is for your life? Explain.

2. Do you show God's love to others? In what ways?

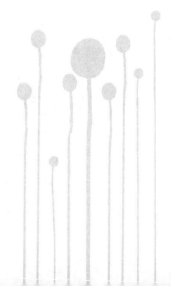

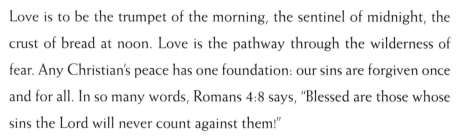

Day 3: My Relationship with Christ
Read Romans 4:7–8

Love is to be the trumpet of the morning, the sentinel of midnight, the crust of bread at noon. Love is the pathway through the wilderness of fear. Any Christian's peace has one foundation: our sins are forgiven once and for all. In so many words, Romans 4:8 says, "Blessed are those whose sins the Lord will never count against them!"

In the classic literary work *Pilgrim's Progress*, author John Bunyan's Christian was, when he arrived at the cross, bent by the weight of his sin, symbolized by a huge bundle under which he had staggered all his life. Then Christian looked up into the eyes of the dying Christ. What he saw was God's gracious love and unconditional forgiveness. The bundle that bent him low all his life suddenly rolled off and was gone. It rolled down the hill of Calvary and was swallowed up in the mouth of the open tomb that Christ left empty when he rose again.

Christian was free! His transgressions were forgiven! His sins were covered! As the psalmist said, "As far as the east is from the west, so far has he removed our transgressions from us" (Psalm 103:12).

There is no more wonderful evidence of God's giving love than the lightness of being we discover when we stand up straight for the first time in our lives, knowing that God has completely forgiven all our sins. The greatest gift is to be free of the curse of our sins forever. Small wonder the hymnist Phillip Bliss wrote:

Free from the law, oh happy condition,

Jesus hath bled and there is remission,

Cursed by the law and bruised by the fall,

Grace hath redeemed us once for all.

—"Once and for All"

Questions for Personal Reflection

1. What evidence do you have of God's giving love?

2. Do you have unconditional forgiveness for others? Why or why not?

Day 4: My Service to Others
Read John 21:15

Every gift is a sign of commitment. Every gift essentially says to us, "I have come to you because the One who gave me to you loves you very much."

Jesus appeared, unexpectedly, to the disciples several times after his resurrection. Christ must have left his friends extremely edgy, popping in and out of their lives as he did. Yet each of his appearances revealed truths necessary to sustain their faith after his ascension.

In John 21:15, Jesus confronted the disciples at the Sea of Galilee where he had first met them some of them. Peter was one of those who long before had been called from the sea to follow Christ because Jesus said he would make them fishers of men. But following the resurrection, Peter was right back where he started, merely "fishing for fish."

So Jesus confronted him: "Peter, do you love me?"

"Yes, Lord," said the fisher-apostle. "You know all things. You must know I love you."

"Well, Peter, if you do love me," said Jesus in effect, "act like you love me—feed my sheep ... serve me."

If giving is the number one evidence of love, giving service must rank close to the top as well. I remember a beautiful Christian, a church member of mine who was very poor. He wanted to give me a present, but had no money. He came to my house, audaciously took all my shoes out of my closet, and began to polish them. He spent the whole afternoon whistling cheerful tunes and polishing my shoes. He loved me. I knew because he served me.

The giving love of God motivates service. Since he gave all, who are we to think that selfish lives, devoid of service, can please him? Love like his—giving, never-quitting love—demands our all. Selective love soon quits loving altogether.

What suitor ever pled, "Darling, here's 83 percent of my heart"? Fractional love is love soon abandoned. Jesus asked Peter heaven's most frequent question: Do you love me?

Questions for Personal Reflection

1. How do you serve God in your daily life?

2. How do you serve others?

Day 5: My Personal Worship
Read Hosea 11:1–8

Hosea 11:1–8 is a magnificent passage that extols love and is written in exquisite poetry. Let us examine each of its rich phrases:

> *"When Israel was a child I loved him"* (v. 1). God likens his giving love to that of a parent loving a baby boy—Israel was God's child, and, like all little children, could not exist without a parent's loving care.
> *"It was I who taught Ephraim to walk"* (v. 3). Pictured here is a parent's joy at a baby's first steps. God gave Israel—here called Ephraim—the gift of maturing, protective love.
> *"I lifted the yoke from their neck and bent down to feed them"* (v. 4). God says that his giving love nurtured Israel in the tender way a mother spoon-feeds or breastfeeds her infant.

Hosea's images of God's love were almost all paternal. But in spite of God's giving love, Israel became a disobedient, delinquent child. Still, in verse eight God lamented: "How can I hand you over, Israel?" God's giving love is a no-quitting love, a love that can only inspire us to exalt him in worship.

At the heart of all worship is love. Those who don't know of God's love will never be inspired to worship. Why? Because they have not seen earth's greatest treasure. Could they but for a moment stand at the cross and gaze into the face of Christ and behold his thorn-crowned smile of grace, then what would be left to do but exalt him? What else could they sing but, "O, come let us adore him"?

Questions for Personal Reflection

1. How do you exalt God?

2. Do you love and praise God daily? Why or why not?

Day 6: Ruth—Love under the Stress of Grief and Separation

Read Ruth 1:16–17

There is no relationship as strong as the fellowship of suffering. Ruth and Naomi went through the pain of widowhood together, clinging to each other when the black mantle of death seemed to shut out all light. Their tears watered their common trust, and it grew. In brokenness their love flourished, proving that we never really know someone until we've wept with them.

The women were penniless. In their utter destitution, Ruth was forced to glean the fields for something to eat. When Naomi left Bethlehem, she was in charge of her life. Now, years later she returned as an exile, bludgeoned by life's brutality. Ruth was an alien, a Gentile Moabitess in a Jewish culture. Suffering made these women friends, but the greatest bond between them was trust.

In this famous passage, Naomi, who had two daughters-in-law, told both of them to return home. Orpah agreed to this (Ruth 1:14), but Ruth did not. Naomi was insistent: "Look, your sister-in-law is going back to her people and her gods. Go back with her" (v. 15). It was impressive that Naomi didn't try to cling to her sons' wives. As an older widow with an uncertain future, she probably would have appreciated their companionship and support.

But Ruth clung to Naomi in love. Naomi had set her free to return to Moab and her family, but Ruth begged: "Don't urge me to leave you or to turn back from you" (v. 16). Thus began a love that would endure across the centuries and enter into the lineage of Christ.

Love as strong as Ruth's is rare. This kind of love always results in service. It is often said that we can serve without loving, but we cannot love without serving. Ruth's love ordered her into the fields to glean. She spent her days bending over to pick the few grains of wheat the harvesters missed. It was wretched work. But when it was over, Ruth's love yielded a harvest of grace.

There are rewards to such love, and Ruth's romance was the final prize:

> *Boaz took Ruth and she became his wife. Then he went to her, and the LORD enabled her to conceive, and she gave birth to a son. The women said to Naomi, 'Praise be to the LORD, who this day has not left you without a kinsman-redeemer. May he become famous throughout Israel! He will renew your life and sustain you in your old age. For your daughter-in-law, who loves you ... has given him birth.... Naomi has a son.' And they named him Obed. He was the father of Jesse, the father of David."*
> —Ruth 4:13–17

Love is strong as steel—the manganese of rugged endurance. It is the platinum heart of all treasure. Love binds those who must live beneath the stress of grief and separation, and says to them, "Weep till you are malleable—God shapes best those whose clay is made soft by tears."

Questions for Personal Reflection

1. Have you ever bonded with someone because you were both suffering?

Explain.

2. Did God's love help you overcome the suffering? Why or why not?

Day 7: Group Discussion

The following questions should take about forty-five minutes to answer and discuss. Each member should answer the first question, leaving the remaining questions open-ended. Everyone need not answer, but be sure all members participate.

1. *Name three gifts, whether spiritual, physical, or relational, that God has given you.*

2. *Do you ever find it difficult to accept God's unconditional love and forgive yourself—as he forgives you? Please give an example.*

3. *If the primary evidence of love is giving, what do you give people you love? In what ways can you serve others to be an example of God's love?*

4. *Does your personal worship reflect the love you feel for God? Do you thank him for his unconditional love for you? What are some ways you could praise him more?*

5.   *What is an aspect from this study that you want to remember and apply to your life?*

6.   *Do you have someone with whom you want to share this lesson? Why? What will you share?*

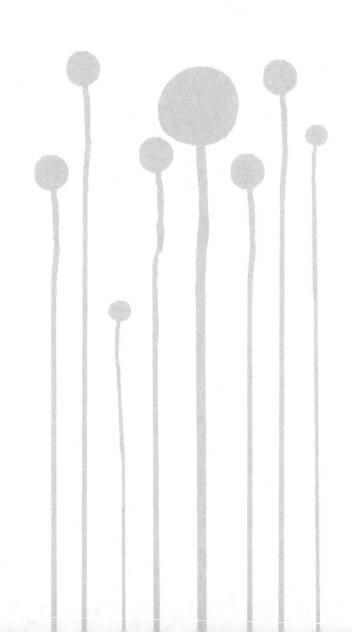

Week 2: Love Forgives

Memory Passage for the Week: 1 John 1:9–10

Day 1: Love Forgives

Facing ourselves is the first fearsome work of being forgiven. Luke 15:11–24.

Day 2: The Purpose of God in My Life

Because mercy is a part of God's nature, he keeps no records of our sins. Love forgives and mercy is in place. Psalm 130:1–4.

Day 3: My Relationship with Christ

The kind of forgiveness Jesus gives cannot be obtained by any kind of moral rules. Instead, it comes softly, like love itself. Acts 13:38–41.

Day 4: My Service to Others

A father's love can only thrive in a family where his children love each other. Genesis 50:15–21.

Day 5: My Personal Worship

Freedom is the only word that can fully describe the state of a person who has been forgiven. Psalm 32:1–2.

Day 6: A Character Study on Jonathan

2 Samuel 1:26

Day 7: Group Discussion

Day 1: Love Forgives
Read Luke 15:11–24

Forgiveness is edgy work! The person extending forgiveness quarrels inwardly over whether or not he or she should extend it. The person needing forgiveness suffers the shame of asking for it, and waiting to be forgiven is downright painful.

The prodigal son in Luke 15 did a noble thing: he faced himself. Perhaps facing ourselves is the first fearsome work of being forgiven. It takes courage to discover the personal need for forgiveness. The hard work is to look in the mirror that is the Spirit of God. At the moment of our confession we are most unlike the conceited queen in Snow White. We know we are not the "fairest one of all." The ugliness of our sin is clear to us. We are needy. We have been self-willed; we have hurt others; we have ridden rough-shod over a whole field of human emotions. But more than this, we owe an awesome debt to God. We have hurt our Father in heaven, and this is the savage center of our sin.

We then make a decision about ourselves. We are sinners, and we need to be forgiven. Our forgiveness is available only in one place. We cannot forgive ourselves all by ourselves, or we would already have done so. The source of our forgiveness can only be found in the hearts of those we've hurt. Our confession needs to lift its downcast eyes toward God, for he, more than all others, has felt the blight of our transgressions. But facing sin means we have to look back into the mirror of condemnation one more time, and then wait. Will those who need to forgive us actually do it? In that question our agony begins.

In the prodigal's case, he had to go home. There alone would the age-old struggle of justice and mercy be resolved. If there was to be life for him; if his heart was to ever beat again, he had to be forgiven. Only his father could do it, just as only our heavenly Father can do it for us.

Questions for Personal Reflection

1. Have you ever had to ask someone for forgiveness? When? Did they forgive you?

2. Have you ever struggled to forgive someone? Explain.

Day 2: The Purpose of God in My Life
Read Psalm 130:1–4

Waiting is the hard work of being forgiven. In Psalm 130:1–2, the psalmist cried for mercy, and in the fifth verse he waited. In the fourth verse he had already confessed that he was not waiting without hope. He knew that God is a forgiving God, and he was certain that his forgiveness would be granted.

But what part does God's forgiveness play in fulfilling God's purposes for our lives? Just this: we cannot work to perform his will while sweltering under the burden of our sins. We must be forgiven, for unforgiven sin dominates the needy soul. While carrying unforgiven sin, we cannot see the good, clear, positive works God performs in our lives.

Guilt is the great debilitator. It paralyzes our desire to do good, whether for God or for those God loves in our world. Guilt exhausts us under the weight of all its grudges. We stagger under self-absorption because we no longer have the energy or inclination to care about others. Guilt causes the best of Christians to avoid Christ and ignore the very best of their friends. It stalks the heart of all relationships, divine or human.

Illustrating it practically, a husband may want to serve his family by making the family's income, caring for the needs of his children, and generally protecting and loving each family member. But if he and his wife have even a small marital struggle, and it is largely his fault, he likely will not prove himself to be a good father and husband until all is forgiven. So, like the psalmist, such a tortured soul must ask for God's forgiveness and wait. When he has been forgiven, he will possess a new lightness of soul that will allow him to fly to his other family responsibilities and accomplish them speedily.

So it is with God. The moment God forgives us, we are instantly free to focus on all that he wants to achieve next in our lives. His purposes are once again sweet and central to our worldview, and no cloud of sin obscures what we are called to do.

Questions for Personal Reflection

1. When was a time you experienced the freeing feeling of being forgiven and letting go of a guilt that had been burdening you?

2. Are you currently experiencing any guilt that is putting a distance between you and a loved one? Between you and God? Explain.

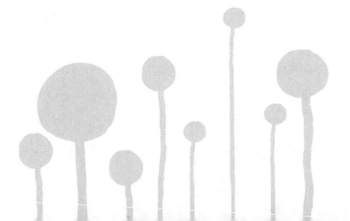

Day 3: My Relationship with Christ
Read Acts 13:38–41

The word *gospel* means "good news." There are many reasons the news is good. It is good because it contains grace, eternal life, and union with Christ. But the best thing about the good news is that forgiveness of sin was immensely simplified when Jesus took upon himself the sacrificial work of the Cross. It was for this reason that Paul cried out in this wonderful sermon:

> *Look, you scoffers,*
> *wonder and perish,*
> *for I am going to do something in your days*
> *that you would never believe,*
> *even if someone told you.*
> —Acts 13:41

And what was this wonderful "something"? The simplification of forgiveness. The law of Moses in the Old Testament did not misunderstand the seriousness of sin, but it did make forgiveness a complex matter of altar slaughter—taking an animal, making a blood sacrifice in the temple, and slaying the animal to get forgiveness. Now, Paul said, Jesus made simple the process of God's loving forgiveness. He died and we are forgiven, merely by asking. The blood atonement is still required, but Jesus took care of it once and for all on the cross.

There is an old hymn, "Nearer My God to Thee!" It is a wonderful song, but the concept is complicated by the distance we put into our relationship with Christ through unconfessed sin. Unconfessed sin can only sing, "Farther My God from Thee!" All sin puts a sense of distance between us and God. We can only be brought near to him through a genuine plea for forgiveness.

Love is the engine that drives God's mighty forgiveness. Love is the energy that sets us free of sin any time we ask.

Questions for Personal Reflection

1. Do you confess your sins in prayer? Why or why not?

2. Do you thank God for Jesus' sacrifice to save us all from our sins? How does this sacrifice make you feel?

Day 4: My Service to Others
Read Genesis 50:15–21

The dying patriarch Jacob begged his family to forgive each other for their past sins. And mercifully they did what he asked. This is no light matter in the history of the nation of Israel. Without Joseph's forgiveness, would the nation of Israel ever have been a possibility? Jacob wanted his family to dwell in peace. He did not want quarrelsome children to allow their arguments to rip apart God's dreams for Israel. If Israel was to avoid becoming inconsequential in human history, it was imperative that each of them grant and receive forgiveness.

How many of God's plans for this world are wrecked when members of his family insist on quarreling with each other? A fighting congregation slurs Calvary's love. It insults the forgiving heart of our heavenly Father.

Wonderful things came about because Joseph forgave his brothers. His own sons, Ephraim and Manasseh, became heirs, along with their ten uncles, in the land that God was about to give them. Israel's family were, in time, forged into a great nation that encountered the world with the greatest single cultural force in human history: Judaism. From Judah—the clan of the forgiving Joseph and his brothers—came a force for learning, law, and medicine, and the mercantile that played a part in world history. Could it be that the whole Jewish structure of civilization was made possible by Joseph's forgiveness long ago?

How much does the kingdom of God suffer when we are unforgiving? Our failure to forgive our brothers and sisters in Christ holds back God's dreams for our future. Let us forgive readily, so that our service to others may be made possible. May God's enterprises never be held back because of our critical spirits.

Questions for Personal Reflection

1. Is there strife and dissension within your family or among your friends? What causes it?

2. What can you do to foster a spirit of forgiveness?

Day 5: My Personal Worship
Psalm 32:1–2

"Blessed is the man whose sin the LORD does not count against him," reckoned the poet (Psalm 32:2). How true! A forgiven soul may enter into the presence of God unobstructed. He or she may meet God not just as forgiven, but as clean. *Clean* is a human synonym for *holiness*. God is not only incapable of sin, he is too holy even to look upon it. But his instant forgiveness of our sins makes it possible for us to approach him freely in our worship. And thus God's forgiveness of us makes possible our fellowship with him.

Worship means loving God. Sin impedes this love.

When we languish under what we will not confess, the only bridge between ourselves and our Father is barricaded. Sin stiff-arms the approachability of God. We can never embrace God while we hold him at arm's length. God's forgiveness gives us elbows; our arms can bend. They can fold around the world at hand.

A child who has disobeyed her earthly father is reluctant to come into his presence. She knows she has wronged him, and while she wishes to feel his embrace and sleep against his chest, she also knows that there is an estrangement between the two of them that cannot be bridged unless she receives his forgiveness. She must ask for it. There lies before such a child the sheepish work of approaching her father and confessing. But after the honesty comes the embrace. Then she falls asleep across his chest. What power can cause such transformation? Grace! All has been removed that was formerly in the way of honest loving.

Questions for Personal Reflection

1. How do you feel after you have talked with God about your transgressions?

2. Do you talk often enough with God? Explain.

Day 6: David & Jonathan—Power of Love between Friends
Read 2 Samuel 1:26

The love between David and Jonathan ranks among the greatest in history. The tale of their friendship is all the more remarkable because it existed under the pall of King Saul's erratic temper and furious jealousy. Saul was Jonathan's father, and he suffered from periods of nearly psychotic rage. During these times of rage, he often tried to kill David.

Consider the requirement life's circumstances had placed on their love: David's best friend, Jonathan, had for a father David's worst enemy. The strongest testament of the strength of their love was exhibited after Jonathan and his father were killed in the battle of Mount Gilboa. There in the still and quiet where so many men had died, David sang to the departed Jonathan,

> *I grieve for you, Jonathan my brother;*
> *you were very dear to me.*
> *Your love for me was wonderful,*
> *more wonderful than that of women.*
> —2 Samuel 1:26

Could there be a finer tribute to the love between friends?

In this day of muddled definitions of love, any kind of same-gender love is often viewed in some homoerotic mode. But David and Jonathan knew the value of the kind of support that comes from finding a lifelong confidant and friend. So many times Jonathan had been his support and had spared David's life from his father's vendettas. David knew that the strength of such an unfailing love between two friends can support us all through life. Proverbs 27:17 reminds us, "As iron sharpens iron, so one man sharpens another."

David had the opportunity to eliminate Saul, his greatest enemy, several times, but he didn't do it. It is not hard to tell why. He believed that Saul had been anointed king, and was convinced that he should not lift his hand against God's anointed (1 Samuel 26:9, 11). He knew that any action he took against Saul would hurt Jonathan, and David was unwilling to do that. David's love for Jonathan caused him to be gracious to Saul even after his death:

> Saul and Jonathan—
> in life they were loved and gracious,
> and in death they were not parted.
> They were swifter than eagles,
> they were stronger than lions.
> —2 Samuel 1:23

Poor are those who must define all love in terms of romance alone. Rich indeed are those who can say, "I have a friend—we love each other." In these friends' confident love every sunrise is welcomed, every crisis is easier, every pain has counsel, and every midnight is safer.

Questions for Personal Reflection

1. Who is your best friend? Why?

2. How has your friend supported you during rough times?

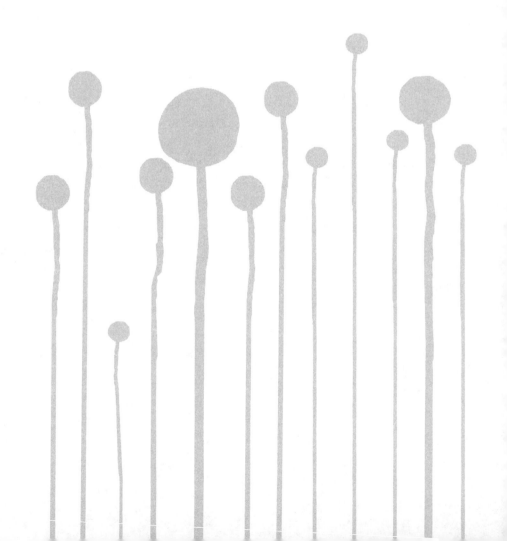

Day 7: Group Discussion

The following questions should take about forty-five minutes to answer and discuss. Each member should answer the first question, leaving the remaining questions open-ended. Everyone need not answer, but be sure all members participate.

1. *Would you describe yourself as a forgiving person? Explain why or why not.*

2. *Is anyone willing to share about a time when it was very difficult to forgive some-one? How did you reach the point of forgiveness?*

3. *If you confess your sins to God, do you feel secure in his forgiveness? Why or why not?*

4. *Why is it sometimes so difficult to forgive? Why do we sometimes falter in our faith that we are forgiven by God?*

5.   Is there someone in your life you need to forgive? Who? Are you ready to do so?

6.   How can this group pray for you to be able to extend forgiveness in the situation mentioned in question 5?

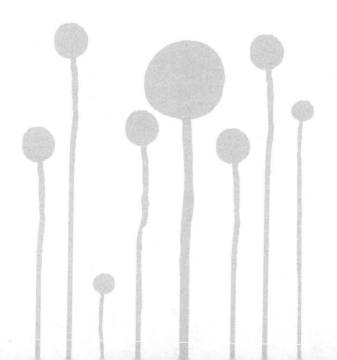

Week 3: Love—The Definition of God

Memory Passage for the Week: 1 John 4:7–8

Day 1: Love—The Definition of God

We are accepted in the beloved not because we deserve God's love, but merely because it is God's nature to love. Hosea 3:1–3.

Day 2: The Purpose of God in My Life

God craves to give us a form that causes all who see us to think of his Son. Isaiah 29:16.

Day 3: My Relationship with Christ

We must not suppose that God ever takes pleasure in our pain. It is not so. Psalm 22:1–5.

Day 4: My Service to Others

How beautiful are those who travel to places of human despair, spreading hope and love as they cry, "Rejoice! He lives!" Isaiah 52:7.

Day 5: My Personal Worship

God rescues us; God keeps us. This alone is worth our praise. Deuteronomy 32:1–4, 10–12.

Day 6: A Character Study on John

1 John 4:7–12

Day 7: Group Discussion

Day 1: Love—The Definition of God

Read Hosea 3:1–3

The very definition of God is love. If 1 John 4:7–8 states this definition, Hosea 3:1–3 demonstrates it. God commanded the prophet Hosea to buy Gomer, his wife, back from a slavery auction block. Gomer had been unfaithful to Hosea, having lived as a prostitute. But Hosea's love for his unfaithful wife was a symbol of God's love for the unfaithful nation of Israel.

The parallels between adultery and idolatry cannot be denied. Just as Gomer had been unfaithful in marriage, so Israel had been unfaithful in her covenant relationship with God. As Gomer had given herself to other loves, so Israel had pursued idols, having abandoned the loving God.

But neither Gomer nor Israel met the castigation of their lovers. In spite of her infidelity, Gomer was loved by her husband. Israel, in spite of her idolatries with foreign gods, was pursued by the unforsaking love of God.

God is in love with us, and his love is totally without merit. His love has nothing to do with neither the good we have done nor the time we have given him in prayer and adoration. God is love! Jesus saves ... period!

How does all of this apply to us?

Grace was how God received us, giving us the forgiveness we never deserved and eternal life we never could have earned by our own moral struggle.

We are accepted in the beloved not because we deserve God's love, but merely because it is God's nature to love. These are ours: this grace, this life.

Questions for Personal Reflection

1. What does "unforsaking love" mean to you?

2. What does "grace" mean to you?

Day 2: The Purpose of God in My Life
Read Isaiah 29:16

Our love for God is manifested in a yieldedness that forbids all back talk. Our love for God says, "Yes, Lord," to whatever he asks of us. Isaiah made the point that it is the potter who forms and the clay that yields. At times the clay becomes stiff in the hands of the potter, and it refuses to be shaped according to his desires. In the same way, at times our self-will stands defiantly before God's all-shaping love, refusing to accept his purposes for our lives.

What then is the next step for such defiant clay? Brokenness. But brokenness is painful for both the potter and his recalcitrant clay. God is a loving parent who does not enjoy breaking his self-willed children. He would much rather they yield to him of their own accord. We must never suppose that the breaking process God uses to change our lives ever brings him any delight. Indeed, he weeps for the process of forcing our stubbornness into usefulness.

On the other hand, being broken is not easy for us either. How much better off we would be if we made joyful yieldedness our immediate response to all God asks. This kind of love is the basis for all of God's dealings with us. He celebrates our instant yieldedness as a triumph of his love. But he is willing—if we will have it no other way—to use a cross to fashion us in the image of his dear Son.

God has no love for crosses. He hated seeing his own Son die on one. But he allowed Jesus that awful and wonderful suffering that redeemed the world, simply because there was no other way to redeem the world. He uses "crosses" to redeem us as well, particularly when there is no other way to redeem us.

Questions for Personal Reflection

1. How do you yield your life to God?

2. How does this make you feel?

Day 3: My Relationship with Christ

Read Psalm 22:1–5

This is the psalm Christ quoted as his last words spoken on the cross. Theologians largely agree that Jesus cried the words, "My God, my God, why have you forsaken me?" because of a great divorce between God and his Son (Psalm 22:1). God, in his holiness, could not bear to look on his Son as he bore the hideous and grotesque sins of humankind in order to save us.

But let us set aside Jesus' quotation of the psalm and examine a single phrase: "I cry out ... but you do not answer" (v. 2). Is not this our frequent lot in life when we face a crisis? As we groan our pleas, it sometimes seems as though our words slide into an abyss, and God—who, in better times, we say is love—seems to ignore us.

At these times when it seems God is silent, I try to remember the promise of Scripture that the Holy Spirit answers our groaning needs not from beyond us, but within us. God is never silent; he is in constant touch with our pain (Romans 8:26; Hebrews 7:25). Our tears are so precious to him that he cries out from within us, constantly making intercession for our sin.

We must remember that what we might interpret as the unresponsive silence of God can be looked at in another way. In hindsight, it is easier to see that God has been with us all along. He was not as silent as we may have supposed. We can remember this to bolster our faith when future "quiet times" arise.

Love is the definition of God. It is a definition we ought to trust, even when we think he is hiding himself from our hurt.

Questions for Personal Reflection

1. Are you able to see ways that God answers your prayers? Give an example.

2. Do you trust God even when you don't hear him? Why is this difficult?

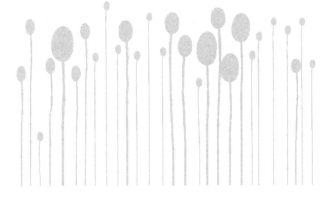

Day 4: My Service to Others
Read Isaiah 52:7

Love motivates the feet of the messenger. The messenger's "going" is just as much a part of the victory of grace as "telling." Going and telling is a part of the Great Commission of Jesus (Matthew 28:18–20). In this passage the two cannot be separated. Most translate the subjunctive force of the Great Commission this way: since you are going into the world anyway, preach the gospel as you go. In other words: all of us are called by God to tell the story; let us do it as a natural part of our everyday involvement. Telling and going are a single action.

There is a tale told of a grateful convert who walked over sixty miles to bring a simple gift to the missionary who led him to Christ. The gift was not expensive, for the poor convert had little of the world's goods to give.

When the missionary saw the simple gift, she received it with joy, but she offered her convert a small rebuke: "You should not have walked so far to bring me this gift."

"Ah," said the convert, "the walk is part of the gift."

This is the spirit of Isaiah 52:7—the "going" is part of the "telling." Going is part of the missionary spirit that permeates the Scriptures. Indeed, the feet are what bring us to the place where we can tell the old, old story of God's love.

Can you remember whom God sent to reveal to you the good news that God was in Christ reconciling? The story they brought you made you alive in Christ, but their walk, their coming to you, was also a part of their gift. How beautiful the message that redeems us, but how beautiful the obedience of those who felt compelled to tell us of his love.

Questions for Personal Reflection

1. Who led you to Christ? Did you ever thank them?

2. Do you ever tell God's story to anyone? Why or why not?

Day 5: My Personal Worship

Read Deuteronomy 32:1–4, 10–12

"Let my teachings fall like rain," cried Moses, "like abundant rain on tender plants" (Deuteronomy 32:2). In verses 10–12 there follows some words of celebration of God who saves us from "a desert land ... a barren and howling waste." God leads us into the glorious promised land of our relationship with him. To be saved is to be released from our commitment to things that don't matter, and to be given a larger commitment to things that do.

But following our salvation, like eagles teaching their young to fly, God pushes us to new, exhilarating kinds of flight, never letting us fall very far before he catches us on his wings. We are secure during every lesson of flight, whether we realize it or not, as we soar into the fullest, loftiest relationship of love.

Moses, who used the book of Deuteronomy as the format for his three farewell addresses to Israel, exulted in praising the gracious love of God. What is the nature of this praise? It focuses on the God who rescues and keeps. Right there where he meets us, he saves us. But that isn't the last we see of him. We soon discover that his saving grace is also his keeping grace. Then we can see what Paul meant in 2 Timothy 1:12 when he said:

*That is why I am suffering as I am. Yet I am not
ashamed, because I know whom I have believed,
and am convinced that he is able to guard what I
have entrusted to him for that day.*

Questions for Personal Reflection

1. What does it mean to be saved by grace?

2. What does being saved mean to you?

Day 6: John—Unforsaking, Lifetime Love
Read 1 John 4:7–12

Yesterday his love was there. Today it meets us at every moment of our need. Tomorrow he will wait for us at sunrise to walk us through the day! We are kept by Christ's unforsaking, lifetime love.

John is often called the disciple whom Jesus loved (John 13:23; 20:2). This is not to imply that Jesus thought less of the other disciples. We can only suspect that it is Jesus' personal response to John's love for him.

Christ's love for John was constant across many decades. This does not mean that John was perfect in every way. He once suggested he be allowed to call down fire on some inhospitable Samaritans (Luke 9:54). For such fiery flights of temper, Jesus nicknamed him (along with his brother James) a Son of Thunder (Mark 3:17). He also had some tendencies toward craving power. He actually asked Jesus to allow him to sit at his right hand when he came into his kingdom (Mark 10:37).

But alongside these more glaring weaknesses, John loved Jesus. When he was an old man on the isle of Patmos, this great love came to fruition. John saw Jesus for the last time. He exulted, "To him who loves us and has freed us from our sins by his blood, and has made us to be a kingdom and priests to serve his God an Father" (Revelation 1:5–6).

In verse 9, he claimed to love Christ so deeply that his love could only be fully demonstrated by the persecution he was undergoing: "I, John, your brother and companion in the suffering and kingdom and patient endurance that are ours in Jesus, was on the island of Patmos be-cause of the word of God and the testimony of Jesus."

John had loved Christ all his life and could exult in his Gospel, the real reason for this love. John quoted Jesus as he said, "Greater love hath no man than this, that a man lay down his life for his friends" (John 15:13 KJV).

John had been captured by Jesus' Calvary love. He was forever after a captive of the heart. John's love would stretch to the limits and would ultimately grow so large, it would define God himself as love in the Word. "God is love" (1 John 4:8). In most ways, so was John.

God's love was the air he breathed, that gave him his voice of praise.

God's love was the water he drank—the fire that warmed his existence in icy storms of hateful persecution.

God's love was God himself—

Constant as the stars—

Warm as the sun—

Steady as the testimony John bore his world.

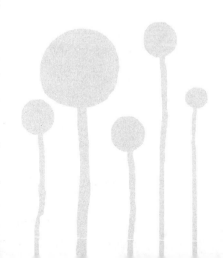

Questions for Personal Reflection

1. Have you ever had a steadfast friend like John? Explain.

2. How does knowing that Christ has a lifetime love for you make you feel?

Day 7: Group Discussion

The following questions should take about forty-five minutes to answer and discuss. Each member should answer the first question, leaving the remaining questions open-ended. Everyone need not answer, but be sure all members participate.

1. *As a child, did you ever disobey and have it backfire? How did your parent(s), your teacher, or another adult discipline you?*

2. *Brokenness is a result of defiant clay. It is painful for both the potter and the self-willed clay. Have you ever experienced tough love? Have you ever practiced tough love? Please give examples.*

3. *Has God ever firmly but gently led you in a direction you were hesitant to go? How did that situation turn out?*

4. *We have all experienced rejection at one time or another. Has anyone ever been indifferent to your love? How did it feel? Have there been times when you have been indifferent to God's love for you?*

5. *Has there ever been a time when you felt that God wasn't listening to you? Explain.*

6. *How do you react when your prayers are not immediately answered—are you able to trust that God still hears you and loves you? Explain.*

Week 4: Love—God's Passion for His World

Memory Passage for the Week: John 3:16–18

Day 1: Love—God's Passion for His World

Even just a small cup of water can irrigate the larger fields of God's harvest. John 4:1–10.

Day 2: The Purpose of God in My Life

It took quite a big fish to convince Jonah that God loved people who Jonah didn't much care for. Jonah 1:1–5.

Day 3: My Relationship with Christ

Christ died for our sins. There are people who don't know this yet. God wants us to get out there and spread the good news. Matthew 28:18–20.

Day 4: My Service to Others

Jesus wants everyone to know that God's love, compassion, and grace has been set loose in the world to comfort all who mourn. Isaiah 61:1–2.

Day 5: My Personal Worship

Worship is the business of heaven. How could one not praise God for salvation? Revelation 7:9–10.

Day 6: A Character Study on Hosea

Hosea 11:1

Day 7: Group Discussion

Day 1: Love—God's Passion for His World

Read John 4:1–10

God's passion for his world is imbedded in the earthiest things. Stand back and look at how God made his entrance into the heart of the Samaritan woman. Jesus asked for a drink, and with just a clay cup of water, God moved into a mountain village. That small cup of water irrigated the larger fields of God's harvest.

God is in love with planet earth. His conquest of love never ceases. Yet he does not storm the planet by conquering continents. Nor does he even evangelize it by zip code and precinct. He has no ad campaigns that inform the world of his good deals for the masses. He is a great God with a small methodology. He unobtrusively shows up among the needy, and usually begins giving to them by asking something of them. He always asks for repentance, of course. But here and there he asks for something simple, yet obliging. In the case of the Samaritan woman, he asked that she extend him a dipping gourd full of cold water.

Common stuff, water. Sixty-two percent of our body is water, and three-fourths of the earth is covered with it. So, it wasn't like he asked the Samaritan woman for a cup of diamonds ... just water. But diamonds, eternal and enduring, were exactly what he gave in return.

Love motivated this diamond-for-water exchange.

"Water," cried her thirsty Lord,
And with reluctance she complied.
He drank, returned the dipper gourd,
She drank. They say she never died.

Questions for Personal Reflection

1. What is something you feel God has asked you to do?

2. How will you respond to his asking?

Day 2: The Purpose of God in My Life
Read Jonah 1:1–5

Jonah's deep-sea experience happened because he refused to love those God loved. How insanely proud are our prejudices? A novel by Jane Austen has a title to which most of us can relate—*Pride and Prejudice*. We are too proud and too prejudiced to offer grace to people we don't like. We all suffer more or less from the same fault. We assume that God is like us. We believe he is unlike our enemies, and that he doesn't like our enemies.

This is how we keep God local. We wall him into our personal world-views. We make him the biggest thing in our province, and we come to think he prefers our zip code to every other zip code in the world. Not only that, but we feel sure that if you ask God, he would tell you that he likes our denomination best and would prefer that other denominations change their foolish dogmas till they more closely match our own glorious doctrines.

Jonah didn't like Ninevites and was quite surprised to find that God didn't feel the same way. In fact, God wanted the Ninevites to repent. Jonah could clearly see that the Ninevites had a lot of repenting to do, but he didn't want credit for the revival God was asking him to hold. He didn't want to see Ninevites get right with God. Jonah would rather have seen God punish the Ninevites for their wickedness. Jonah felt that the best way to help some people quit sinning was just to zap them!

But in the belly of the fish, Jonah discovered a great truth: his enemies were not God's enemies. God was in love with everybody and, in fact, loved Ninevites as much as he loved Jews. One little burp later, Jonah was on the way to help some of God's friends, whom he had never much cared for, to have a chance at growing a relationship with God.

Questions for Personal Reflection

1. Have you ever felt God loves some people more than others? Explain.

2. When do you find it most difficult to love all people equally?

Day 3: My Relationship with Christ

Read Matthew 28:18–20

My relationship with Christ is secure. He proved on the cold, windy day he died that his love for me was real. Of course, I never would have known it happened except that Matthew, among others who saw it happen, wrote it down in his wonderful biography of Christ. There are many things that make me trust Matthew and the other Gospel writers. Most of them died as martyrs still sticking to what they wrote in their Gospels. People sometimes die for lies they believe to be true, but they won't knowingly die for lies.

There is one other incontrovertible witness to their truth—they all died a long way from where they met Jesus. One has to ask, "What would cause Matthew, Peter, and John to die so far from their homelands?" What was it that caused them to abandon dusty and provincial little Galilee? They moved far away from home to tell the Good News till they were finally arrested and martyred. Obviously, they had met in Jesus one who would live at the core of their belief system and motivate them to leave their families and businesses and never look back with any regrets.

God's compassion for the world was their only motive. Somehow Jesus managed to forge their bravado into real courage and send them halfway around the world to die for their transforming stories. If Jesus could forge these ordinary souls into such nomadic transformers, I can only conclude that Matthew 28:18–20 must also be my calling as well.

His will, his call, and his commission are mine. Wasn't it wonderful of Matthew to give us his account of the good news? It really is world-changing stuff.

Questions for Personal Reflection

1. Have you ever gone out of your way to tell the Good News? Why or why not?

2. Have you ever had to sacrifice anything to spread God's Word? Explain.

Day 4: My Service to Others

Read Isaiah 61:1–2

Is it not altogether wonderful that God, who is himself secure in the heavens, should care about things so remote and far away as earth? Is it not amazing that God, who transcends flesh and has no nervous system, should care about earth's major preoccupations: pain, death, imprisonment? Jesus became a human being, and wasn't it wonderful of God to take this bold step and give himself an alimentary canal, a nervous system, and a circulatory system that would in time allow him to bleed and thus redeem us? You can trust a God who willingly made it possible for himself to bleed to death, just to be sure no one would ever be able to accuse him of not understanding human existence.

God's love is his passion for his world. He serves prisoners, the poor, and the brokenhearted. God has made sure that everyone gets the good news. Of course, the truth is that we are the newsboys, who make sure that the word gets out and that no one ever dies not having heard of his love. This is how we serve the world he loves. We're the information people; we are the World-Wide-Webbers, publishing the worldwide hope.

We are the trustees of the most remarkable news. God, for no good reason that will profit him, actually cares about us. This news is so good that without it, the bad news would be very bad: the universe would be a madhouse without scheme or key. Believe it because there is nothing else of worth to trust. Believe it because it is not only true but it is the most beautiful truth that can be imagined.

Questions for Personal Reflection

1. How do you help to spread God's Word?

2. With whom do you share his message of love?

Day 5: My Personal Worship
Read Revelation 7:9–10

Notice that in the book of Revelation the union of time and eternity has come! God is love, and those who are redeemed of all ages are in love with him. The divine romance has come to fruition. And notice what the redeemed of all ages do when they enter the celestial presence: they praise. Those who find no joy in adoration here on earth will find heaven to be quite the opposite. Worship is the business of heaven. The Second Coming is the downbeat for an eternity of praise. My book *The Finale* imagines the Second Coming breaking forth into praise:

> *The long awaited prince had come ...*
> *The liberated prisoners sang ...*
> *The Golden Age has dawned upon the grave of time and we are free!*
> *We lay aside the chains of our humanity.*
> *The Singer comes to save the remnant of the age.*
> *The gates fling wide!*
> *The banner waves above the Troubadour of Life,*
> *Astride a steed of light!*
> *He comes! He comes! The Blind can see!*
> *The halt march perfectly!*
> *The Prisoners are free!¹*

With such love watching the borders of eternity, praise is the very least we can do. Is there any reason that our personal worship should not join the adulation of those in Revelation who stand in his glory at last, overwhelmed by his grace forever?

Questions for Personal Reflection

1. Do you try to make your personal worship special to God? How?

2. What do you most look forward to in heaven?

Day 6: Hosea—Love, the Unrelenting Pursuit of God

Read Hosea 11:1

God is the hound of heaven. He pursues us to the grand encirclement of his love. God said to Hosea, "Go take to yourself and adulterous wife and children of unfaithfulness, because the land is guilty of the vilest adultery in departing from the LORD" (Hosea 1:2). From this commandment began the story of one of the most unusual writers among the Minor Prophets of the Old Testament. Hosea married a woman whose adulteries were met by his unconditional love for her. Hosea loved Gomer and the children of their marriage, not all of whom seem to have been biologically his (Hosea 1:9), but his love was not enough to call Gomer back from her adulteries. Finally, after Gomer's desertion, God commanded Hosea to go find Gomer and show his love to her yet again. Hosea found Gomer, brought her back from a slavery auction block, and showed her his love once again (Hosea 3:2).

This story focuses on Hosea's undying love for his wife. But it is really a metaphor for God's love for a faithless nation. God loved Israel to what would seem the very limits of his tolerance. But Israel continually turned away from God in a foolish affair with idolatry and indulgence. In spite of all this, God was most reluctant to give up Israel. He cried with a broken heart in Hosea 11:1–3:

When Israel was a child, I loved him,
And out of Egypt I called my son.
But the more I called Israel,
the further they went from me.
They sacrificed to the Baals
and they burned incense to images.
It was I who taught Ephraim to walk.

God pursued Israel, and Israel was indifferent to his love. Perhaps there is no greater sin against the heart of a father than to spurn the majesty of his love. This spurning seems all the more tragic because of the sense of brokenness that was revealed as a loving God reached, and Israel rebelled. "How can I give you up, Ephraim?" was the heart cry of a holy God who was in agony over human indifference to his love (Hosea 11:8).

"How can I give you up?" is a question God must still ask every time we insist on having our way, leaving him weeping over our indifference. Yet nothing will ever stop God's all-pursuing love.

God's love is in the quiet tread of his footsteps when we think we are walking all alone. We are pursued by the power of God's immense affection. He is in love with us. Therefore we feel him all around us even when the world tells us we're in this life all alone. Ever onward he pursues us, chasing us at last into his divine embrace. We are surrounded by grace, irresistible and eternal. We are ensnared, and the entrapment is our glory.

Questions for Personal Reflection

1. Think of something you have done that you feel might have made God weep

for you. What was it?

2. In what ways do you feel God's love most strongly?

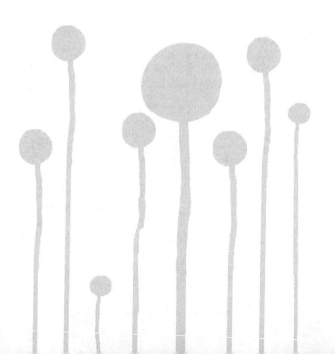

Day 7: Group Discussion

The following questions should take about forty-five minutes to answer and discuss. Each member should answer the first question, leaving the remaining questions open-ended. Everyone need not answer, but be sure all members participate.

1. *What are you most passionate about?*

2. *Has pride ever stood in the way of your love for someone? How about prejudice? Explain.*

3. *Whose passion for Christ has inspired or is currently inspiring you?*

4.   *What does the Great Commission mean to you? How do you see it being played out around you? How does it apply to your own life?*

5.   *Read Revelation 7:9–10 again. What do you imagine heaven to be like?*

6.   *God's love for us is unforsaking, lasting a lifetime. Who in your life has been your friend the longest? What has sustained that friendship over so many years?*

Week 5: Love—The Unconditional Longing of God

Memory Passage for the Week: Song of Songs 2:4

Day 1: Love—The Unconditional Longing of God

God is in love with us, and he loves us with an active and ardent passion. Exodus 19:3–6.

Day 2: The Purpose of God in My Life

Christ enters our hearts and places his calling—our purpose—to publish the good news that God is, in Christ, loving us. Song of Songs 8:6–7.

Day 3: My Relationship with Christ

In our sin we did nothing to prompt God's unconditional display of divine affection. Yet, amazingly, there was Jesus, loving us as though we deserved it. Romans 5:5–8.

Day 4: My Service to Others

Hell is real, but it is not God's wish that anyone go there. God wants us all to have a new heart and a new spirit. Ezekiel 18:30–32.

Day 5: My Personal Worship

God loves us unconditionally. We should never stop celebrating that love in our worship. Joel 2:12–13.

Day 6: The Parable of the Prodigal Son

Luke 15:11–32 (TLB)

Day 7: Group Discussion

Day 1: Love—The Unconditional Longing of God
Read Exodus 19:3–6

God is not passive in his romance with humankind. Do you object to the word *romance* as somehow too human and too shallow to be applied to God? It is a reasonable objection. Human romances often prove fickle and divorce-court temporary, but consider the pure energy in the word *romance*. God is in love with us, and he loves us with an active and ardent passion.

In Hungary long ago there was a young woman named Elizabeth and a young crusader named Louis. They fell in love, and their love was so celebrated in Hungarian history that it still remains one of the great love affairs of all time. Elizabeth said that her passion for Louis knew no bounds and that every moment apart was a moment wasted. Over the course of time, Louis went to serve in the Crusades and was lost in war. Elizabeth at first pined deeply and lived in black and somber seclusion. But God was ever near to her during her bereavement, and soon Elizabeth began to turn to Christ the lost affections she once gave to Louis. She never married again, but her love for Christ made her one of the greatest ministers of all time. She lived in her day as a sort of Mother Teresa of Hungary, bearing the Word of God in counsel and healing and converting the lost. Ultimately, she learned that the love of God was the most superior and most undeserved love in the world.

Moses understood the deep passion God has for his people. He knew well before Elizabeth of Hungary that God's great love has about it an unconditional and undeserved grandeur. If God could quit loving, he would quit being God. Therefore Moses wrote these words of God: "You yourselves have seen what I did to Egypt, and how I carried you on eagles' wings and brought you to myself.... Although the whole world is mine, you will be for me a kingdom of priests and a holy nation" (Exodus 19:4–6).

God loves unconditionally!

Questions for Personal Reflection

1. Do you ever wonder how God can love you unconditionally no matter what you do? Explain.

2. Do you feel you can love everyone unconditionally? Why or why not?

Day 2: The Purpose of God in My Life

Read Song of Songs 8:6–7

It is not difficult to understand why St. John of the Cross, widely regarded as one of the greatest poets of the Spanish language, was inspired to write his beautiful collection of prayerful poems titled *Flame of Love*, for as Solomon said, "[Love] burns like a blazing fire, like a mighty flame. Many waters cannot quench love; rivers cannot wash it away" (Song of Songs 8:6–7).

There is great passion in God's saving love. It not only saves us, it daily reveals his purpose in our lives. His love is the fuel and energy of our calling.

Paul celebrated this purpose-revealing, energy-driving love in what some have called a believer's victory hymn:

> *Who shall separate us from the love of Christ? Shall trouble*
> *or hardship or persecution or famine or nakedness or danger*
> *or sword? As it is written:*
> *"For your sake we face death all day long;*
> *we are considered as sheep to be slaughtered."*
> *No, in all these things we are more than conquerors through*
> *him who loved us. For I am convinced that neither death nor*
> *life, neither angels nor demons, neither the present nor the fu-*
> *ture, nor any powers, neither height nor depth, nor anything*

else in all creation, will be able to separate us from the love of

God that is in Christ Jesus our Lord.

—Romans 8:35–39

We are owned, managed, and in debt to the incendiary passion of God, a love unquenchable for the life everlasting:

Oh Love that will not let me go,

I rest my weary soul in thee.

I give thee back the life I owe,

That in the blessed crimson flow

My life may richer, fuller be.[2]

—George Matheson

"Oh Love That Will Not Let Me Go"

Questions for Personal Reflection

1. When do you feel you need more passion and purpose just to get through each day?

2. Do you remember to ask God for more passion and energy? Why is it important for you to do so?

Day 3: My Relationship with Christ
Read Romans 5:5–8

Was there ever love like this love which Jesus gives us?

God did indeed demonstrate his unconditional love for us in that while we were yet sinners, Christ died for us (Romans 5:8). In his dying we were cemented in that love which fixes us forever in the Beloved. And our relationship with Christ is secured in that Calvary love that wakes us every morning to ask, "Was there ever love like this?"

There is an old story that exists in several forms, but the one I like the best tells of a little boy carrying a light bag across his shoulder. The bag was full of strange flutterings, which did not escape the notice of an old man who passed the boy on a narrow bridge. The old man was nearly past him when intrigue and compassion overcame him, and he spoke to the boy quite abruptly, "Whatcha got in that bag, sonny?"

"Nothin' but a bag full of sparrows," replied the boy.

"Whatcha gonna do with those birds?" probed the old man.

"I'm gonna torture them, pull out all their feathers, and then when they can't fly anymore, I'll feed 'em to the cat."

"How much would you take for all of 'em?"

"Oh, 'bout two dollars," said the boy.

The old man reached in his pocket and pulled out two dollars. "Here," he said. The boy took the money and handed him the sack of sparrows.

The old man opened the bag, and all the birds bolted, feathers thrashing as they flew into the sunlight.

Imagine that God met Satan on the bridge between worlds. Satan had a sack on his back, and God said, "What's in the sack, Satan?"

"Humanity," Satan replied.

"What are you gonna do with them?" God asked.

"I'm going to force them to live lifetimes of brutality and pain, and then when they're all worn out, I'm going to throw them into hell."

"What will you take for them?" asked God.

"Just the life of your Son," Satan replied.

"Done!" said God, and as the hammer rang out upon the nails, God opened the bag and set humanity free.

Unconditional love behaves that way: while we were yet sinners, Christ died for us.

Questions for Personal Reflection

1. Do you feel you can sin and still be loved? Why or why not?

2. What must you do to secure God's unconditional love?

Day 4: My Service to Others
Read Ezekiel 18:30–32

What is to be the heart of our service to others? To fall in love with love and to preach the unsearchable riches of Christ. Our service is to inform the world that God is after them, and beg them to come soon to his love. It is to preach, "Rid yourself of all the offenses you have committed, and get a new heart and a new spirit" (Ezekiel 18:31).

I have often wondered if Ezekiel could have had the full light of the New Testament if given the chance to stand back and be lost in rapture while gazing at Calvary love. To see the cross high and lifted up makes the unconditional love of God very visible. Jesus hung on Calvary to speak the message, "Rid yourself of all the offenses ... and get a new heart and a new spirit" (v. 31). Then he faced the cross as the world's most dramatic example of unconditional love.

> *Life's lessons come in wood and steel,*
> *And hope is born where vengeance cries.*
> *Forgiveness grows where God must feel*
> *What tears the soul and crucifies.*
> *Because of your deep guilt and sin*
> *My life was counted loss;*
> *I shuddered in the April wind,*
> *I knew the chafing cross.*

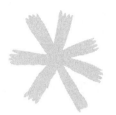

Earth's epoch hourglass spilling time
Has measured centuries since then;
You played your part in cosmic crime.
You need a cosmic friend. [3]

Questions for Personal Reflection

1. Do you ever feel that God is longing for a closer relationship with you?

Explain.

2. Do you ever long for a closer relationship with him? Why or why not?

Day 5: My Personal Worship
Read Joel 2:12–13

Ritual sometimes has a tendency to get away from the truth it was formed to emphasize. Liturgies are written largely by poets to celebrate, in beautiful words, the unfailing love of God. So we repeat them, and repeat them, and repeat them. But before long their beauty becomes callused with coarse familiarity. Then we repeat dead words, and we cannot feel the love and life they communicated to us when we were younger and those words were newer.

Israel had rituals for rending their garments, but alas, they mouthed old words they never meant. God had become a theological discussion in Israel. They could talk about him for hours and never feel a thing for him. It had been a long time since they had felt anything for God. So the prophet Joel encouraged them: "Rend your hearts and not your garments" (Joel 2:13). We must let God into our lives, and quit meeting him for church while refusing to speak to him in the streets. God does not want us to talk about him anymore unless we're actually thinking about him.

God's love is too almighty, too gracious, and too compassionate to be a mere subject in theology. He loves us unconditionally. He wants us to love him the same way in return. We should never stop celebrating that love in our personal worship.

Listen to the poet call you to God's unchanging heart of love:

Could we with ink, the oceans fill,

And were the skies of parchment made,

Were every stalk on earth a quill,

And every man a scribe by trade,

To write the love of God above,

Would drain the ocean dry.

Nor could the scroll contain the whole,

Though stretched from sky to sky.[4]

—"The Love of God"

Frederick M. Lehman

Questions for Personal Reflection

1. Do you feel your personal worship has become routine? Explain.

2. Do you take church rituals for granted during worship? If so, how can you reenergize your worship?

Day 6: The Parable of the Prodigal Son

To illustrate a point, Jesus told this story in Luke 15:11–32 (TLB):

A man had two sons. When the younger told his father, "I want my share of the estate now, instead of waiting till you die!" his father agreed to divide his wealth between his sons.

A few days later this younger son packed all his belongings and took a trip to a distant land, and there wasted all his money on parties and prostitutes. About the time his money was gone a great famine swept over the land, and he began to starve. He persuaded a local farmer to hire him to feed his pigs. The boy became so hungry that even the pods he was feeding the swine looked good to him. And no one gave him anything.

When he finally came to his senses, he said to himself, "At home even the hired men have food enough and to spare, and here I am, dying of hunger! I will go home to my father and say, 'Father, I have sinned against both heaven and you, and am no longer worthy of being called your son. Please, take me as a hired man.'"

So he returned home to his father. And while he was still a long distance away, his father saw him coming, and was filled with loving pity and ran and embraced him and kissed him.

His son said to him, "Father, I have sinned against heaven and you, and am not worthy of being called your son—"

But his father said to the slaves, "Quick! Bring the finest robe in the house and put it on him. And a jeweled ring for his finger; and shoes! And kill the calf we have in the fattening pen. We must celebrate with a feast, for this son of mine was dead and has returned to life. He was lost and is found." So the party began.

Meanwhile, the older son was in the fields working; when he returned home, he heard dance music coming from the house, and he asked one of the servants what was going on.

"Your brother is back," he was told, "and your father has killed the calf we were fattening and has prepared a great feast to celebrate his coming home unharmed."

The older brother was angry and wouldn't go in. His father came out and begged him, but he replied, "All these years I've worked hard for you and never once refused to do a single thing you told me to; and in all that time you never gave me even one young goat for a feast with my friends. Yet when this son of yours comes back after spending your money on prostitutes, you celebrate by killing the finest calf we have on the place."

"Look, dear son," his father said to him, "you and I are very close, and everything I have is yours. But it is right to celebrate. For he is your brother; and he was dead and has come back to life! He was lost and is found!"

Questions for Personal Reflection

1. Describe a time you struggled to keep from being jealous of someone.

2. How often do you thank God for the people in your life?

Day 7: Group Discussion

The following questions should take about forty-five minutes to answer and discuss. Each member should answer the first question, leaving the remaining questions open-ended. Everyone need not answer, but be sure all members participate.

1. *Who in your life would you be willing to give up anything to save?*

2. *Where do you see unconditional love in the world today? Where is unconditional love needed the most?*

3. *How is unconditional love evident in the parable of the prodigal son? With whom in this parable do you identify most?*

4. *Do you feel that love is alive and active in the worship of your church or small group? Explain. What are you most thankful for about your church or group?*

5. Do you carry the love and closeness you feel when you fellowship with other Christians and with God throughout the rest of your week? In what way(s)?

6. What is one thing from this study you want to remember and apply to your life?

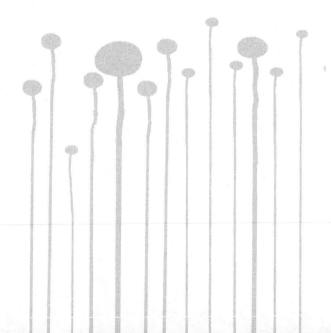

Week 6: Love—The Incarnational Force of God

Memory Passage for the Week: Galatians 4:4–5

Day 1: Love—The Incarnational Force of God

In uniting the fruit of the Spirit passage (Galatians 5:22–24) with the "love chapter" of the Bible (1 Corinthians 13), we find a guide to the Christian life. 1 Corinthians 13:1–7.

Day 2: The Purpose of God in My Life

Not only are we to love the stranger in our midst, but we are to love him or her as we remember times when we, too, were in need of love. Leviticus 19:33–34.

Day 3: My Relationship with Christ

God loves us so much that he allowed the godhead to be incarnated in human flesh in order to end our alienation with him. Colossians 1:19–22.

Day 4: My Service to Others

Foot washing is the service Jesus rendered the night before he died, showing that no service born out of love is beyond our dignity. John 13:1–8.

Day 5: My Personal Worship

Joy is contained in the partnership we hold with God. Joy and worship! 2 Corinthians 5:17–21.

Day 6: Verses for Further Reflection

Day 7: Group Discussion

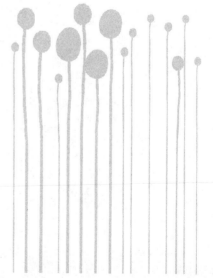

Day 1: Love—The Incarnational Force of God
Read 1 Corinthians 13:1–7; Galatians 5:22–24

Two of the greatest passages in a Christian's development are Galatians 5:22–24 and 1 Corinthians 13. What is so interesting about these two passages is that one is completely contained in the other. In uniting the fruit of the Spirit passage with the love chapter of the Bible, a flawless guide is obtained to the Christian's inner life. Consider these two wonderful passages, juxtaposed in their glorious relatedness:

GALATIANS 5:22–23	1 CORINTHIANS 13:1–7
1. Love	Does not seek its own, is not selfish or self-centered.
2. Joy	Love does not rejoice in iniquity but rather rejoices in the truth.
3. Peace	Love is not easily provoked, but is serene and stable.
4. Patience	Love suffers long, perseveres, and is patient.
5. Kindness	Love is merciful, thoughtful, and concerned; it envies not.
6. Goodness	Love is great, gracious, and generous; it is kind and good.
7. Faithfulness	Love thinks no evil but has faith in God and others.
8. Gentleness	Love is humble and gentle; it does not vaunt itself.
9. Self-Control	Love is disciplined and controlled; it does not behave unbecomingly.

Love is the first fruit of the spirit. It is well-placed at the head of the list, for it permeates everything. Somehow if we live a life of love, the other virtues will attend us all the days of our lives. Love is the key that unlocks the entire fruit basket of Galatians 5:22–23.

Questions for Personal Reflection

1. What is the most important aspect of love to you?

2. What is the hardest part of love?

Day 2: The Purpose of God in My Life

Read Leviticus 19:33–34

Give Leviticus 19:33–34 your heart, and soon it will own your soul. This splendid passage falls out in a triptych of three panels, each speaking their own glory:

1. "The alien living with you must be treated as one of your native-born" (v. 34). Here God brought up a perennial old problem: the issue of insiders and outsiders. Insiders are those who belong; outsiders are those who don't. Insiders get all the good deals; outsiders don't. Insiders control; outsiders are controlled.

    As if this were not enough, there also exists a feeling among insiders that outsiders need to be further outside than they already are. If only they were far enough outside, then they would never have access to any insiders. There exists a further notion that insiders shouldn't be hurt by life, but outsiders don't matter. The worst case scenario happens when insiders come to a joint opinion that outsiders should just be killed to put an end to the social tension altogether.

    God, in this passage, was acting to clear up the tension between insiders and outsiders. Aliens (outsiders) must be treated just like those who were native-born (insiders)—end of argument, beginning of love.

2. "Love him as yourself for you were once aliens in Egypt" (v. 34). Here is a novel idea: love people who are in the outsider category. Why? Because, God said, you were once outsiders in Egypt. The Israelites knew how rotten it felt to be outsiders. God challenged them, since they, too, had felt the pain, they should never make anyone, anywhere, go through what they went through.

3. "I am the LORD your God" (v. 34). This last phrase was God's signature. Who told us to love outsiders? Well, we all know who said so—God! The Lord! If he takes such an interest in loving outsiders, it must be a good idea for everyone.

Questions for Personal Reflection

1. How often do you reach out to someone in need?

2. Are you willing to help others even if they are from another church or from another country? Why or why not?

Day 3: My Relationship with Christ

Read Colossians 1:19–22

Colossians 1:19–22 contains the grand interrogatives of God's saving work in Jesus Christ. Read the passage and watch them unfold.

1. **Who** is the keeper of this grand incarnational force? Why, it is God who, in his own wonderful imagination, conceived of something as powerful as the incarnation and was willing that all the Godhead should dwell bodily in Christ.

2. **Why** would God put such celestial and redeeming machinery in place? Because God is in love with people who really don't love him all that much. To overcome the problem of human disinterest in his love, he came to make peace. Those who didn't love him were reconciled, and their reconciliation was the entire reason for this "divine romance." With every drop of blood that fell, God said, "I love you, I love you, I love you."

3. **When** did God affect this great redeeming plan? At the very time we were in need. At the time when we were alienated, indeed even we were his enemies. Galatians 4:4 said God did his reconciling work when the time was exactly right, in *plenitudo temporis* (in the fullness of time). It was exactly the right time for us.

4. **For what purpose** did God do all this? Here's the most
    wonderful part of it all: so he could present us as completely
    holy in his sight, without blemish and free from every accu-
    sation. Isn't it wonderful that Jesus lived a completely sinless
    life? But God has arranged it so that we look morally just like
    Jesus because of his work on the cross.

The architect of this wonderful reconciliation is love—love, the stuff
of God; love, the very definition of God; love, the incarnational force of
God.

Questions for Personal Reflection

1. What is the only thing you have to do to be reconciled with God?

2. What is the effect of this reconciliation in your life?

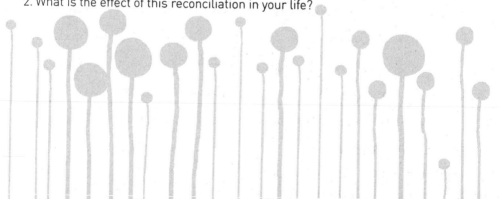

Day 4: My Service to Others
Read John 13:1–8

What would cause the King of heaven to wash the feet of earthlings? One thing alone could make it happen: love. If love is the engine of John 13, then humility is the output. Jesus washed the disciples' feet and, in so doing, made it clear that the servant is not greater than his Lord, and neither is he that is sent greater than he that sent him.

But what is humility? Is it the ability to put oneself down by sheer self-loathing? No, there is something else involved. Humility does not involve making a decision because our self-esteem is so low we could go ahead and wash people's feet. Humility is not arrived at through some come-downance in our pride.

I know of only one authentic path to humility. It is to stand next to Christ and see that by comparison with the King of heaven, we have a lot of reasons to be humble. This means that nothing he did could ever be too lowly for us to do. If he could bind his waist with a towel, maybe we could learn the art as well.

Like Peter, would we object to ever permitting the King of heaven to serve us? Actually, it is already too late for that. Jesus has fully redeemed us by purchasing for us a grand liberty paid for by his own execution on the tree.

Now then nothing is beneath our dignity.

Now then all things he might ask of us are reasonable.

Now then, having seen his purchase of love, we gladly take up our own basin and towel.

Questions for Personal Reflection

1. Think of a time when you humbled yourself before someone. How did it make you feel?

2. Have you humbled yourself before God? Why or why not?

Day 5: My Personal Worship

Read 2 Corinthians 5:17–20

Ambassadorial status is the final work of love. God is re-creating the world by the sheer force of love, and we can be his representatives.

1. God is making new creatures out of old sinners (2 Corinthians 5:17). This is not just a giant, celestial re-treading operation. God is creating a species that has never before been. All who come to him trade sins for grace and come out as a new creation. The newness overwhelms the believer for the sheer joy of the differences seen between what was and what is.

2. God has made these new creatures fellow business partners in extending the kingdom of God (vv. 18–19). This means that the joy of world changing is not just a lot of fun God keeps for his own amusement. We who have become new creatures are to work with God in the creation of more new creatures. Joy is contained in the partnership we hold with God! Joy is the result of God's creative work! Joy and worship!

3. We gained ambassadorial status when we were made new (v. 20). Ambassadors are those who live in one realm while representing the business of another. Our home address is now one realm away, and we are here in God's beloved

world, trying our best to help him claim it before both realms become one. We are citizens of heaven, working to make earth look a little more like it before history is concluded.

We are under obligation to reconcile the world unto God, and the joy of this immense calling makes every sunrise brighter.

Questions for Personal Reflection

1. How can you use love to extend the kingdom of God?

2. What is the reward you will gain from helping to reconcile the world?

Day 6: Verses for Further Reflection

Matthew 22:37: Love the Lord your God with all your heart and with all your soul and with all your mind.

Luke 6:27: But I tell you who hear me: Love your enemies, do good to those who hate you.

John 13:34: A new command I give you: Love one another. As I have loved you, so you must love one another.

John 14:15: If you love me, you will obey what I command.

John 15:9: As the Father has loved me, so have I loved you. Now remain in my love.

Romans 5:5, 8: And hope does not disappoint us, because God has poured out his love into our hearts by the Holy Spirit, whom he has given us.... But God demonstrates his own love for us in this: While we were still sinners, Christ died for us.

Romans 12:9: Love must be sincere. Hate what is evil; cling to what is good.

Galatians 5:13–14: You, my brothers, were called to be free. But do not use your freedom to indulge the sinful nature; rather, serve one another in love. The entire law is summed up in a single command: "Love your neighbor as yourself."

1 CORINTHIANS 13:1–13

This passage is perhaps the greatest passage on love ever written. It was written to the Corinthian church—a church desperately in need of love.

If I speak in the tongues of men and of angels, but have not love, I am only a resounding gong or a clanging cymbal. If I have the gift of prophecy and can fathom all mysteries and all knowledge, and if I have a faith that can move mountains, but have not love, I am nothing. If I give all I possess to the poor and surrender my body to the flames, but have not love, I gain nothing.

Love is patient, love is kind. It does not envy, it does not boast, it is not proud. It is not rude, it is not self-seeking, it is not easily angered, it keeps no record of wrongs. Love does not delight in evil but rejoices with the truth. It always protects, always trusts, always hopes, always perseveres.

Love never fails. But where there are prophecies, they will cease; where there are tongues, they will be stilled; where there is knowledge, it will pass away. For we know in part and we prophesy in part, but when perfection comes, the imperfect disappears. When I was a child, I talked like a child, I thought like a child, I reasoned like a child. When I became a man, I put childish ways behind me. Now we see but a poor reflection as in a mirror; then we shall see face to face. Now I know in part, then I shall know fully, even as I am fully known.

And now these three remain: faith, hope and love. But the greatest of these is love.

Questions for Personal Reflection

1. What can we learn from the "love chapter" (1 Corinthians 13)?

2. How does being loved by God make you feel? How can you share his love?

Day 7: Group Discussion

The following questions should take about forty-five minutes to answer and discuss. Each member should answer the first question, leaving the remaining questions open-ended. Everyone need not answer, but be sure all members participate.

1. *Which verse of the verses for further reflection was your favorite? Why did this particular verse stand out to you?*

2. *Who in your life most embodies love to you? What does this person do that is especially loving?*

3. How is God's love described in 1 Corinthians 13:4-7? Have you ever experienced this kind of love in a relationship?

4. First Corinthians 13:13 says, "And now these three remain: faith, hope, and love. But the greatest of these is love." In Galatians 5:22, "love" is listed as the first fruit of the spirit. Why do you think love is considered the most important of all these attributes?

5. *What are some opportunities in your life in which you could serve as God's ambassador to the world?*

6. *Is love a fruit of the Spirit that is blossoming in your life, or is it one that you need to pray about in order for it to develop?*

ENDNOTES

1. *Calvin Miller,* The Finale *(Downer's Grove, IL: InterVarsity Press, 1979), 147.*

2. *George Matheson, "Oh Love That Will Not Let Me Go" [written 1882],* Baptist Hymnal *(Nashville, TN: Convention Press, 1975).*

3. *Calvin Miller, "When First I Reckoned with His Love," from* An Owner's Manual for the Unfinished Soul *(Wheaton, IL: Harold Shaw Press, 1997), 65.*

4. *Frederick M. Lehman, "The Love of God," 1917, arranged by Claudia L. Mays,* Songs That Are Different, *1919.*

PRAYER JOURNAL

Use the following pages to record both prayer requests and answers.

PRAYER JOURNAL